Hi, I'm Jack. I go to college.

Every week Mum gives me some money for bus fares and food.

This is my family.

We would all like to have more money.

Dad works long hours. He earns most of the money for the family. He pays all the big bills.

Mum works part time. She doesn't get paid
very much. She spends her money on
everyday things. She gives me an allowance
and Nick gets some pocket money.

My sister Kim is training to be a hairdresser. She works in a salon and goes to college one day a week. She gets paid as an apprentice. Kim gives Mum some money because she still lives at home.

Nan lives alone. She just gets her pension. She is always hard up. She doesn't complain.

These are my brothers.

Nick is twelve. He has his pocket money every week. He does a few odd jobs to get some extra cash.

Colin has just lost his job at the warehouse. He's really fed up. He gets Jobseeker's Allowance while he looks for work.

If I had a bike I could get a paper round. And I could cycle to college...

If my family gave me a few quid each I would have enough to buy one.

I ask Mum. She says,"I already give you what I can. All my money goes on food shopping and stuff for the house and you kids. I only get the minimum wage you know! And I'm trying to save up a bit for a holiday."

I talk to Dad about giving me some money.
He says, "You must be joking, lad. Everything
I earn goes back into the house. There's all
the bills - rent, gas, electric, phone... Then
there's the car. Petrol is expensive."

I try my sister. She tells me, "I have to get to work, buy clothes and food, get stuff for college *and* I give money to Mum. If I had any spare cash I'd buy loads of clothes and go out clubbing every weekend. I wouldn't give it to you!"

I talk to Nick. He tells me he's spent all his
money on a new game for his games
console.

And then I try Colin. He's not happy. "Jobseeker's Allowance is a joke! It's not enough to live on. And I need money to look for work. I need a mobile phone too. I can't even afford to go out with my mates."

I've just lost my job in case you hadn't noticed!

Last of all I go to see Nan. She says, "I would really like to help, Jack. But I only have my pension you know. It's not very much to pay all my bills and buy food. It's just as well I don't have to pay for my tablets any more."

But Nan has an idea...

When I get home Mum has another idea. She works at a care home.

"I've been thinking," she says. "They want someone to do odd jobs at the care home. Why don't you pop in and ask about it? It won't be much money, but it's a start."

What do you think?